Caroline Arnold

Wiggle and Waggle

Illustrated by Mary Peterson

![Charlesbridge] Charlesbridge

For Matthew—C. A.

For my digging and singing partner,
Jonathan—M. P.

Text copyright © 2007 by Caroline Arnold
Illustrations copyright © 2007 by Mary Peterson
All rights reserved, including the right of reproduction in whole or in part in any form.
Charlesbridge and colophon are registered trademarks of Charlesbridge Publishing, Inc.

Published by Charlesbridge, 85 Main Street, Watertown, MA 02472
(617) 926-0329 • www.charlesbridge.com

Library of Congress Cataloging-in-Publication Data
Arnold, Caroline.
 Wiggle and Waggle / Caroline Arnold; illustrated by Mary Peterson.
  p. cm.
 Summary: Two worms who are best friends have fun together as they tunnel their
way through a garden. Includes facts on how worms help plants grow.
  ISBN 978-1-58089-306-0 (reinforced for library use)
[1. Worms—Fiction. 2. Best friends—Fiction. 3. Friendship—Fiction. 4. Gardens—
Fiction.] I. Peterson, Mary, ill. II. Title.
PZ7.A7346Wig 2007
[E]—dc22   2006020948

Printed in China
(hc) 10 9 8 7 6 5 4 3 2 1

Illustrations done in pencil on paper and painted in Photoshop
Text type set in Goudy and Comic Sans; display type hand-lettered by Mary Peterson
Color separations by Chroma Graphics, Singapore
Printed and bound by Regent Publishing Services
Production supervision by Brian G. Walker
Designed by Susan Mallory Sherman

Contents

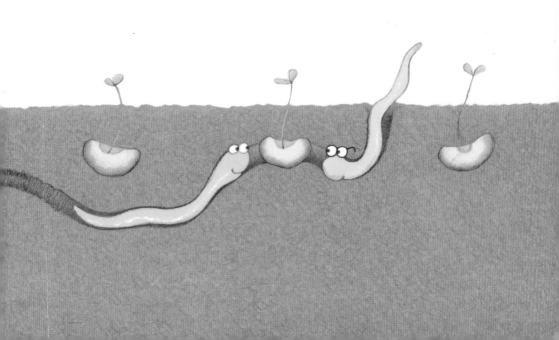

A Digging Song

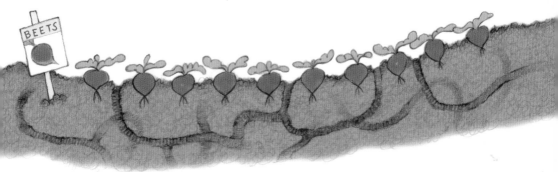

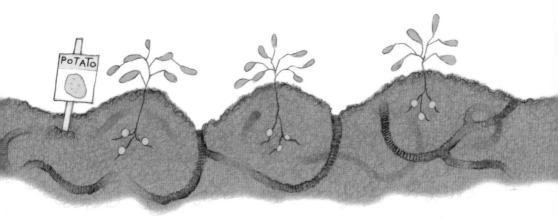

Wiggle and Waggle were worms.
They lived in the garden.
All day long they dug in the dirt.

7

They slid between the beets.
They looped around the carrots.
They pushed under the peas.
Their tunnels gave the plants room to grow.

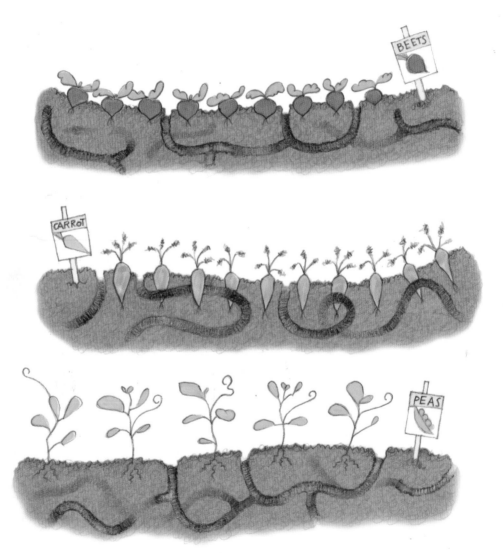

"This is hard work," moaned Wiggle.
"We will never be done."

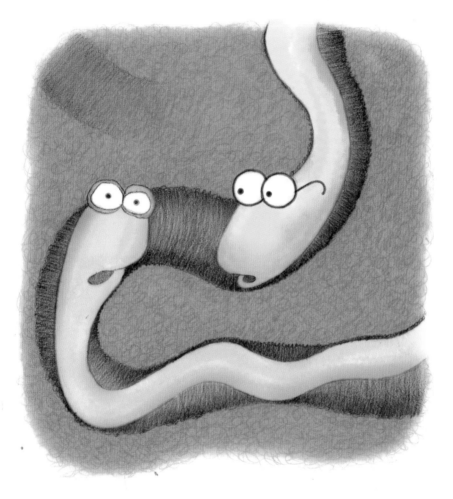

"Let's sing as we dig," said Waggle.

Wiggle sang the high notes.
Waggle sang the low notes.

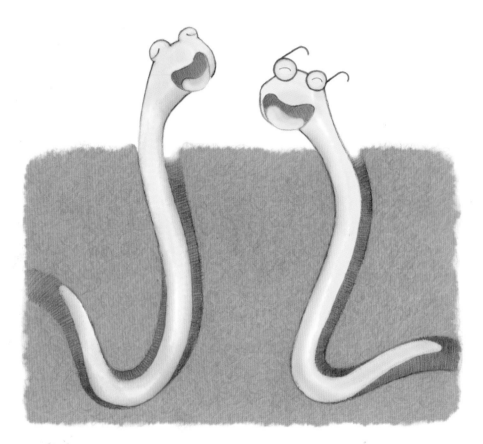

We wiggle and waggle, squiggle and squirm.
Digging in dirt is the life of a worm.
We dig and we sing all day long,
Our wiggly, waggly, gardening song.

They dug long tunnels,
short tunnels,
fat tunnels,
and thin tunnels.

Soon all the garden rows were done.

"What a good song," said Wiggle.
"It made our work go faster."
"Let's sing it one more time," said Waggle.

We wiggle and waggle, squiggle and squirm.
Digging in dirt is the life of a worm.
We dig and we sing all day long,
Our wiggly, waggly, gardening song.

"That was fun," said Wiggle.

"Yes," said Waggle. "We are a good team."

"I agree," said Wiggle.

"Let's dig again tomorrow."

A Big Rock

Wiggle liked to dig fast.
He zoomed around the corn.
He zipped under the beans.
He zagged between the potatoes.
Sometimes Wiggle forgot to look
where he was going.

BUMP! He hit something hard.
"Ouch!" he cried.
A rock was in his way.

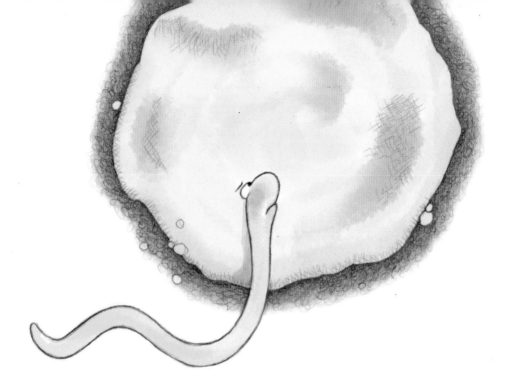

Wiggle tried to go over the rock.
It was too high.

He tried to go around the rock.
It was too wide.

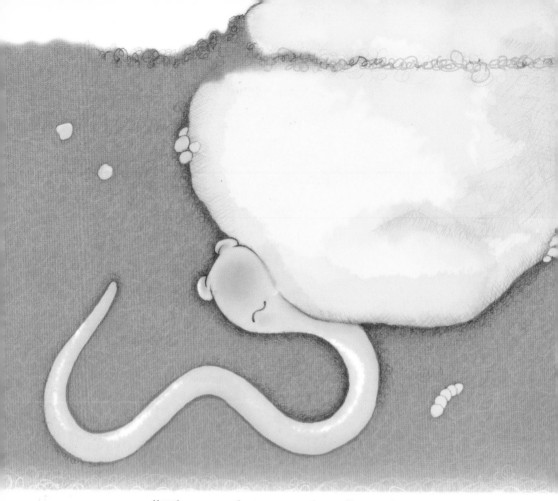

"This rock is too big," said Wiggle.
"I will have to move it."
Wiggle took a deep breath.
He pushed hard.
The rock did not budge.
Wiggle tried again.
Still the rock did not move.
"This rock is stuck," said Wiggle.

"Let me help," offered Waggle.
Wiggle and Waggle leaned against the rock.
"One, two, three, PUSH!" said Waggle.

Wiggle and Waggle pushed.
The rock began to roll.

"Hooray!" shouted Wiggle.
"Let's do it again. One, two, three, PUSH!"

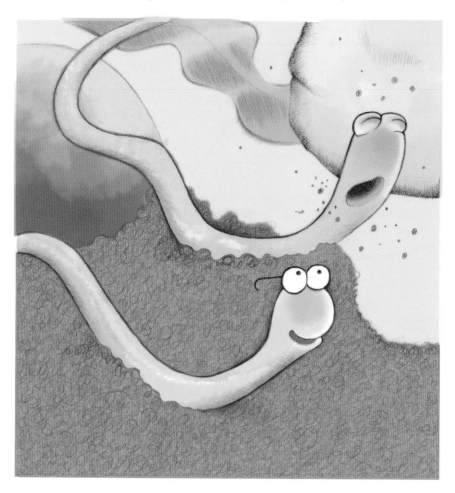

Little by little they rolled the rock
out of the garden,
down the hill,
and into the ditch.

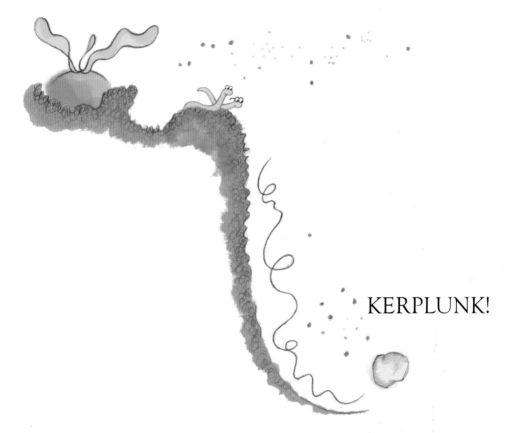

KERPLUNK!

"Thank you," said Wiggle.
"Now I can dig fast again."
"I was happy to help," said Waggle.
"That's what friends are for."

A Day Off

Wiggle and Waggle worked hard every day.
The plants grew big and strong.
"Let's take a day off," said Wiggle.
"How about a picnic?" said Waggle.
"I will bring dirt rolls and bug juice," said Wiggle.
"I will make a mud pie," said Waggle.
Wiggle and Waggle packed their food.

They climbed to the top of the hill.
"Too windy," said Wiggle.

They went to the woods.
"Too shady," said Waggle.

They slid to the pond.
"Too many bugs," said Wiggle.

Wiggle and Waggle looked up at the sky.
A big dark cloud was coming their way.
Rain began to fall.

"We can't stay here," said Waggle.
"It is too wet."

Wiggle and Waggle hurried back to the garden.
They slid under a pail.
"Let's wait here," said Wiggle.

Splish, splash. The rain poured down.
"I am hungry," said Wiggle.
"Have a dirt roll," said Waggle.
Soon all the dirt rolls were gone.

Pitter, patter. The rain poured down.
"I am thirsty," said Wiggle.
"Have some bug juice," said Waggle.
Soon they drank the last drop.

Plip, plop. The rain poured down.
"Something sweet would taste nice," said Wiggle.
"Have some mud pie," said Waggle.
Soon they ate the last slice.

"What a good picnic," said Wiggle.

"Yes," said Waggle.

"We picked the perfect spot."

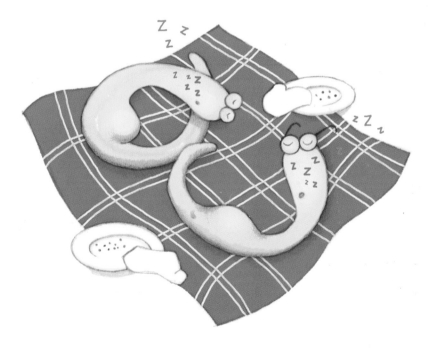

Too Much Mud

The rain stopped at last.
Everything was soaked.
A big puddle filled the middle of the garden.
Wiggle and Waggle slid across the wet dirt.
They looked into the puddle.

They saw the sky.
They saw the garden plants.
"Look!" said Wiggle.
"We can see us."
"We are muddy all over," said Waggle.
"What a mess!" said Wiggle.

"I have an idea," said Waggle.
"Let's go for a swim."
He jumped into the water.
SPLASH!

"Last one in is a rotten egg!" shouted Waggle.
Wiggle jumped in after him.
SPLASH!
"I will beat you to the other side!" he yelled.
Wiggle swam on his back.
Waggle swam on his side.
They raced across the puddle.

Soon the sun came out.

The air grew warm.

The puddle grew smaller.

"It is time to get out," said Waggle.

Wiggle and Waggle dried off in the grass.
"Look!" said Wiggle.
"No more mud."

"Yes," said Waggle.
"Rain is good for the garden.
It also helped us get clean."

A Good Job

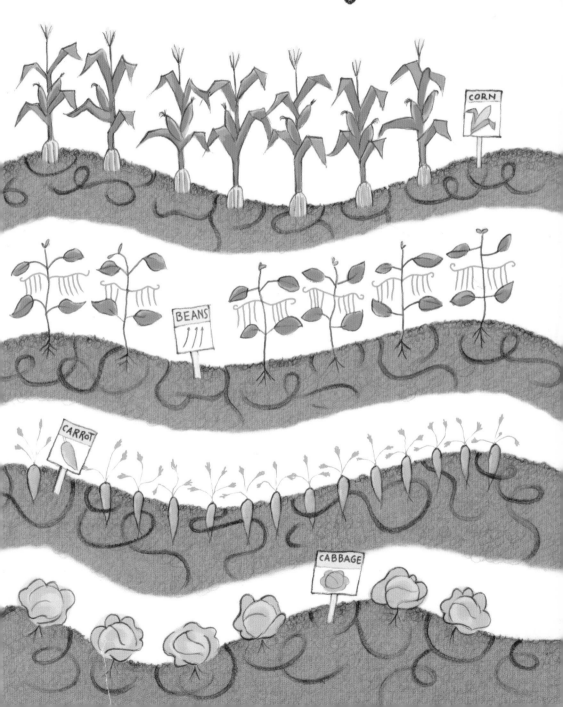

The summer days passed.
Wiggle and Waggle dug and dug.
The corn grew big.
The tomatoes grew fat.
The beans grew long.
They were ready for picking.

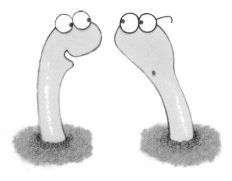

"We did a good job," said Waggle.
"Now we can rest until spring."
"Yes," said Wiggle, "after I dig one more tunnel."
"Can I help?" asked Waggle.
"No," said Wiggle.
"I am making a surprise."

Wiggle dug deep in the dirt.
Waggle waited while Wiggle worked.

At last Wiggle was done.
"Follow me," he said.

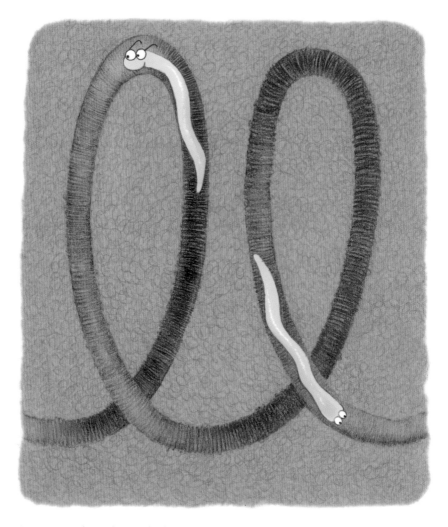

Wiggle slipped into a tunnel.
Waggle slid after him.
They dipped and climbed.
They did fancy twists.
"This is odd," said Waggle.
"The tunnel shapes are just like letters."

He slid through the tunnel again.
He said each letter out loud.
"W-I-G-G-L-E. W-A-G-G-L-E."
"Oh!" he shouted.
"The tunnel spells our names."
"Yes," said Wiggle.

"What a nice surprise," said Waggle.

They slid through the tunnels one more time.
"I like to dig," said Wiggle.
"Me too," said Waggle.

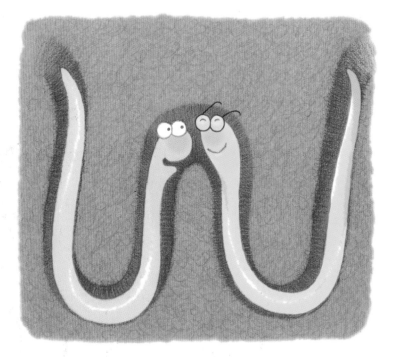

"Let's do it again next year," said Wiggle.
"We can zip and zag and zoom again."
"Yes," agreed Waggle. "It will be fun."
"We will make the best garden
ever!" said Wiggle.

Then Wiggle and Waggle opened their mouths and sang.

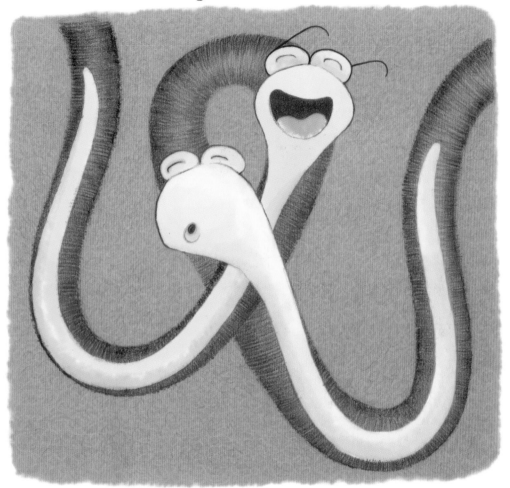

We wiggle and waggle, squiggle and squirm.

Digging in dirt is the life of a worm.

We dig and we sing all day long,

Our wiggly, waggly, gardening song!

How Do Worms Help Plants Grow?

Worm tunnels help air and water get into the soil.
This makes the soil loose.
Then plant roots can grow more easily.

Worms eat old leaves and other plants.
Their body waste contains food that plants need.
It fertilizes the soil.

Worms mix up the soil as they dig.
They carry dirt from the top of the ground
to the soil below.
This way the plants always have a new supply.

Worms help make garden soil healthy.
They help plants grow big and strong.

Fun Worm Facts

There are more than two thousand kinds of worms in the world.

The smallest worms are only one inch long.

The biggest worms can grow to twenty-two feet.

Worms do not have lungs. They breathe through their moist skin.